Tumblehome

poems by

Susan Jaret McKinstry

Finishing Line Press
Georgetown, Kentucky

Tumblehome

ACKNOWLEDGMENTS

"Knowing" was first published in *Plain Songs II,* edited by Rebecca Harrison, 2000.

I am grateful for so many people who inspire and encourage me. To my brother
Peter Jaret, always my first call and first reader. Cathy Yandell who always makes me
better, Sue Wilds for long friendship, Leslie Schultz, model of poetic generosity, and
my poetry group Jane Sarles Larson, Orick Peterson and Sharol Nau. The intrepid
Ireland travelers: archaeologists Stephen Mandal and Muiris O'Sullivan, Debbie
O'Brien, driver Brendan Murphy, and adventurers Roger and Mary Ashley, JoAnne
Ball, Julie Schoenig and Chris Ball, Mary and Mats Brenner, Joel and Nancy Dimsdale,
Paul Fraker and Cecelia Spitznas, Barb Waugh, and Randy and Margaret Nesse. My
students at Carleton College, who keep me thinking. And always Stephen, Ryan, Dylan
and Ellen, who love words, music, and one another—what gifts you are, every day.

Publisher: Leah Huete de Maines
Editor: Christen Kincaid
Cover Art: Susan Jaret McKinstry
Author Photo: Mark S. McNeil
Cover Design: Elizabeth Maines McCleavy

Order online: www.finishinglinepress.com
also available on amazon.com

Author inquiries and mail orders:
Finishing Line Press
PO Box 1626
Georgetown, Kentucky 40324
USA

Contents

I. Leaving Coins

Leaving Coins

She hands me a small tin of coins,
asks if I will leave them
along my overseas travels,
in memory of her father.
I never knew him. I only know
his suicide shadows her heart.
I do not ask enough questions
about the task, her hopes.
Like a foolish character
in a fairytale or quest,
I simply set out, tin in hand.

The west coast of Ireland
holds history, religion, myth
in each rocky hillside, deep pool
and cloud-shaded lake.
Fairy gifts and sacred objects
festoon small trees: Virgins, angels,
bells, Covid masks hang together
to mark centuries of belief and hope.
In a great stone circle
on an improvised altar
of small offerings, I leave one coin.

The Valley of Madness. The monastery of exile.
The monk's fishing house cleverly built
over a rushing river to feed the abbey.
The portal tomb pointing upward
in a vast field of limestone slabs—
each proof of human yearning to grasp
something beyond limited life. Coins for all.

When the tin was empty, I came home,
quest done. Trying to explain
in words and iPhone photos
what each place meant and felt,
I understood grand attempts:
each giant stone laid atop another
says as much about faith as engineering;
these ancient sites chastise our casual cries
and highlight our small, essential gestures;

the quest is always more about what
the quester learns than what
the task asks. My brother's ashes
drift about the world's seas. Grief
is always precise and dispersed.

Coins glint from a rock, quiet lake,
flashing stream, tangled garden, crashing sea,
a trail of tiny crumbs to follow,
a small bright bit of human memory offered
to the magnificent, indifferent world
that goes on regardless.

Bird's-Eye View
Grange Stone Circle, County Limerick, Ireland

Easy to miss the Grange Stone Circle
if you drive as fast as winding roads permit,
distracted by sheep and patchwork green hills.
Leave the car, climb the small rise through the gate
to the great circle spread before you.

Over one hundred standing stones encircle
a flat half-acre of grass. Look across,
walk the circumference, see how level it lies
four feet down as if obscured
from careless eyes. Try to imagine why
they smoothed such rocky ground,
transported and raised huge slabs of stone
by horse and man and persistence
into the perfect circle visible in aerial photos.

Bird's-eye view makes it obvious
but they were not birds, those builders,
and no hills or tall trees overlook the spot.
Answers vanish over four thousand years
even as massive rocks erode and fall.

The archaeologist lays a rope
across the wide space, hands you
unlabeled pictures of unfamiliar ruins,
asks you to order their making, try
to distinguish Neolithic from Bronze from Iron,
set your sites down where they belong
on geologic time's long expanse.
You see human time's tiny place,
ages of human life clustered in a brief stretch
surrounded by so much unknown.
You look around the enclosing circle.
The stones stand, waiting.

One waist-high stone has become an altar
of coins, keys, flowers, pebbles, rosaries,
rings, fairy ribbons, a falcon feather.
Check your pockets. You might add something to it,
though you can't explain why, before you leave.

Fishers of Men
Cong Abbey, County Mayo, Ireland

Fast-running rock-filled River Cong
rises from deep limestone fissures,
grows wide, brims with salmon and trout,
flashes past the 12th century Cong Abbey,
disappears after a brief mile above ground.

A narrow stone bridge crosses the water
to the 15th century monk's fishing house
mid-stream on its level stone platform.
The roof is gone. The doorway's perfect arch,
graceful straight walls and squared chimney
prove the mason's craft, hands and eyes
working such obdurate matter for months,
working to make his vision true. After all,
monks need to eat. Grumbling bellies
divert even the holiest prayers
from the heights of heaven.
Privation may be the devil's bait.
The river is rich with fish. How best
to worship and honor God's plentiful gifts?

The monk dreams of stone floors
smoothed even, each flat slab matched
to its neighbor, together holding the house
dry and ready over the river. Past the door's inviting arch,
a flawless fireplace to ease winter's chill.
Between, a trapdoor to lower lines into the river.
In summer, fish seek shade under the house;
in winter, slowed waters between the rock columns
draw fish near as monks wait warm by the fire.

When fish bite, the monks pull a bell-line
to tell their brothers that dinner has come today,
carry their dazzling catch across the straight stone bridge
and through the woods to their Abbey home.
God provides. A monk builds a house
that feeds spirit and flesh, grace and ingenuity
embodied in each stone,
the hook and line of faith and need
sunk deep and risen together
like a small miraculous river.

Oratory
Gallarus Oratory, Dingle Peninsula, Ireland

On a hill near Ballyferriter
in the Dingle Peninsula's western tip,
its curving roads and unmarked turns,
jagged stone walls threading
over billowing green hills,
a perfect small stone building
like an upturned boat, keel
pointing to air's immensity,
upends sea and sky to recreate
the work of reaching heaven.

Arched like the children's game
of turning hands into church,
stone fingertips touch gently
over the empty space.
Stone walls curve smoothly inward,
gravity and craft perfectly met
in each obstinate rock's rounded nest
against its unyielding neighbor
to form the beehive-shaped whole.

Inside, the world contracts
to this damp shelter, stone-smell, age-dense,
the low door darkened by visitors,
the narrow high window gives slight light
but—stories say—promises heaven
to those who can squeeze through it.
Imagine the monks at prayer, wondering
if their words transcend the dim place
or echo endlessly around the curved walls.
Wondering if here oratory becomes song,
sails into the heights of heaven,
the depths of the sea turned sky,
structure and voices and space
together shaping salvation
into a corbelled miracle of cut rocks
perfectly balanced on one another
through ten centuries of Irish storms.

Tucked into the landscape,

the shape of those held hands,
that hive, that upturned boat,
gives unbelieving us a taste
for all we do not understand
even as we experience it
in each cool, smoothed stone
we touch with yearning fingertips.

Portal

Poulnabrone Dolmen, The Burren, Ireland

On a high field of limestone slabs
scattered like small coffins,
Poulnabrone, the portal tomb, points
up to the heavens or down to death.

Four straight stones tall as doors
balance a large capstone roof.
Two people might lie along its length,
a limestone bed for mythic Irish heroes
angled into the star-sparked sky,
or lie under it undisturbed by gnawing animals,
recurrent human plunderers, errant tourists.

Six thousand years ago Neolithic people
hauled massive stones from elsewhere
to this desolate place of limestone and wind,
heaved them somehow to form the tomb,
used it for 600 years, then stopped.
Cleaned bones of young men, women
and children, malnourished, work-worn,
lie mixed together in the prominent tomb,
fine objects set among their partial remains.

The back door is fallen. A rope keeps us out.
The silence is eerie, footing treacherous.
Small flowers peer from gaps between stones:
yellow spots of eye-bright, nodding blue harebells,
the spiked seed claw of bird's-foot trefoil
signaling fall, their fragile persistence
vivid against the heavy stones
of that vast, barren landscape
of rocks as far as we can see.

In a hospice bed four thousand miles away,
my ex-sister-in-law slowly leaves her body.
It is a terrible process. No wonder
I think about the portal tomb.

High on a wind-beaten hill, visible for miles,
holding ancient bones, it seems to promise

care for the dead. For some need beyond the body,
whatever it might be, marked by human tenacity:
heave massive stones into a high doorway,
and still see that tiny bright flowers can thrive
in deep gaps between inhospitable rocks
that we must cross with caution and awe.

Telling the Bees

"When the Queen Died, Someone Had to Tell the Bees"
(New York Times headline, September 13, 2022)

The royal beekeeper
taps the hive and says:
the Queen is dead.

The bees will do
what bees do. Swarm
around the dripping frame,
drift over his bare hands
and face, listen,
then settle back busy,
task and status clear
in their gathering.

In London's Green Park, bees float
over rows of strewn flowers
and massed mourners,
pause at bright clothes,
find fragrant living plants,
alight, collect what they need,
head home to the hive.
Their hum runs under
the human hush, endless selfies
and bouquets, coins, cards,
letters, drawings, photos:
Elizabeth as young Queen
and serene elder in purple
gazes straight at the shifting crowd
of mourners unsure of what to do.

The Queen is dead. Her body
in a red-and-gold flag-draped coffin
processes, slow and heavy,
from Balmoral to London
by plane, glass hearse, by gun carriage
pulled by 142 Royal Navy men,
placed by eight synchronized pallbearers
to lie in state. People swarm
around barricaded streets

to be part of this history,
to wonder at her work,
wonder what comes next.
Fretfully busy, we know so little
about our purpose.

Bees know. The Queen bee
is dedicated to the hive,
the hive to her for life.
Why not tell the bees?
Wouldn't we like to believe
that shared acts matter,
that we might somehow ensure
sweet honey will go on flowing
into a future that even now,
as we stand uncertain
of the necessary steps,
is gathering around us?

The Barn of Your Love

Pomp and solemnity mark the funeral
for a 70-year reign, each detail quietly
planned for years, practiced to perfection.

The mourners decorous and sincere,
cherubic young choristers rapt,
the readings profound enough
to fill the hallowed spaces
of the ancient abbey
and maybe catch the ears
of the illustrious dead long buried
under its smooth stone floors.

Broadcast live around the world,
the event reaches millions.
In all that care for every aspect,
no one alerted the stenographer
to the language of common prayer.

"Come holy God and Phil our hearts
with the barn of your love"
the archbishop implores. Perhaps
Philip can hear, can join his wife
in their now unbodied selves
after her awful isolation
at his funeral. Barn indeed,
that vast arched space. Perhaps
the carved horses can come alive,
nostrils flaring, tails twitching
with impatience to canter away.

Another stenographer hears
"the bomb of your love armor"
and stone-armored knights nod,
smug and shielded from the blast
that heaven or hell shall bring.
Barn or bomb, she's seen it all.
Bring it on. The Queen is ready.

How does the world say farewell
to such an age-old public figure?

The archbishop knows: the service ends,
"and Jesus Christ our lord oh man"
and oh I agree, there is little else to say.

Like That

Flaggy Shore, County Clare, Ireland

To catch a thing,
form the amorphous
in words, metered lines
down a white page,
perhaps rhymed,
starts and stops
neatly punctuated.

To catch a thing,
name some thing
like, highlight like
as disruptive caesura,
swift-diving line break,
enigmatic flight,
join this to that.

To catch a thing,
turn things to signs.
Loyalty of paired swans drifting
over their mirrored selves
on a dark Irish lake.
Grief of a sole swan, neck bowed
to empty water.
Chill of impending rain.
Burnished decay of autumn.
Silvered blue of a storm-lit lake
echoing iridescent air

like nothing else.
Metaphor is not the end.
Literal swans still mate and float,
seasons leave and return.

Can a poem catch your heart?
If poetry works like this—
like a key, like a window,
like an x-ray or telescope,
what was hidden now in your sights,
held still and ready for what you will do—
what will you do with that?

II. The Restless Necessary

Tumblehome

1. *"Sadness is no more than a bit of acid transfixed in the cerebellum."*
    —Alan Lightman, *Einstein's Dreams*, 1992.

Galway August gray stone
walls stone sky
stand over rushing
water over rocks between
bridges channel fast full
constant like sadness

notes echo down
narrow carless medieval
streets music stirs
eddies clusters dispersions
like a lung filling emptying
tourists workers coins
voices lilt tangle
bodies bump
swerve into the dark

to the sea looking out always looking out

one abandoned building
painted bright with
poem or warning: 'still just
another empty house'

maybe streets are narrow
to keep them home

at the end
of the street sea
goes to
gray sky

2. *"'John Reney's boats'—that means something. … Because they
    were good boats and blessed with luck."*
    —Galway City Museum display, *Connaught Tribune,* 1954.

Galway hooker full-size
gaff-rigged wood-masted

black-sailed black boat floats
between three floors
of the small museum

stormy day tourists glance over
balconies staircases edges drop
coins into the empty
replica of John Reney's
last hooker *Truelight* 1922

black and white photos
flat-capped Galway fishermen
shawled women fish-filled baskets
children ragged proud
stare at the photographer
boats safe on shore

livelihood risk transport
shaped for rough seas
curves wide then narrows
like a ribcage
like the coast like
an embrace promising
so much yet

what can stand such
wind-driven sky-darkened
relentless beating
men in small boats
yearning for home?

3. *"The true believers in this superstition would not go out to sea if they*
    would meet the red-haired woman."
    —Galway City Museum label, 2016.

carry a piece of mountain ash or
rowan tree know if the boat is
lucky know the sea takes
all she ever wants
all

did my kinswomen hide
red hair under scarves pray

they not scuttle the ship fear
their own power?

put twigs in strong pockets
or worn shoes to keep safe
watch the sky
waterproof
meager luggage with Irish sap

hope for land

4. *"How do you know but ev'ry Bird that cuts the airy way,*
    Is an immense world of delight, clos'd by your senses five?"
    —William Blake, *Marriage of Heaven and Hell*, 1790-93.

as if gravity is not enough
as if I choose between
earth and air as if
the sea beckons me to join
as if invitation is all
to fly out and away

August afternoon solstice-dark
Cliffs of Moher erased
weather wind so
relentless a body becomes light

look out clutch black slab
see nothing know
the invisible is there
crowds gather look into
emptiness the sheer edge
of expectation

old man huddled
in black trash bag
plays accordion
fingers feel keys
notes vanish to wind

flare of sight
moss-covered cliffs fall
white gull held

buffeted before dark cliff
spun into deep fog
sharp insistent wind
erases all

wind-flung people take
selfies stumble on
fog-slick stones sheer drop
like time made physical like
all we fear all
we cannot see

from the road straight
stone walls climb green hills
black-faced sheep brown cows
grey Connemara ponies
great tumbled rocks
disappear into fog

drive through tiny Kilvane
brief bright-lit window
radio broadcaster
scratches his chest leans
into microphone looks
into space throws his voice to
everyone anyone out there
as *Nick Hawkes Craft Butcher*
closes his red shop door
glimpse gone

in Ireland death would be
craft in Ireland
obscured cliffs bring
some form of seeing
in Ireland people facing
absence hope

5. *"It's too late for expectations."*
    —Overheard, Corrib River Path, Galway, August 2016.

Corrib River hotel window hours pass
birds walkers runners pass

morning swans teach dark cygnets the tide
afterschool children burst bicyclists zip
high-heeled girls stumble on cobblestones
night drunks sing and silence
yellow lifesavers hang
on rock walls along the river's
white rapid rush to sea
beyond my square of sight light
shifts builds darkens returns

red flowers over gray stone
clouds float regroup move
across the river in windows
people appear go come back
swan gull bike cloud face voice
lone child in small kayak
lifejacket bright face tense
mother runs on shore calls
he tries for small harbor spins
back in current and away

beat

father tows an empty kayak
paddle extended struggles
spins lets go
two kayaks disappear
after the child

window empty

6. *"Time will tell, it always does."*
    —*Dr. Who,* Season 9, Episode 5, 2015.

bridge harbor tide slows opens
people lean cast pose
billowing wedding gowns
white swans drift gulls call
photos families someone

will catch the boy the father

will catch up the mother

will catch up breathless will

all become a story another story
of Galway bay will

end safe home

7. *"and may you in your innocence*
   sail through this to that"
   —Lucille Clifton, "blessing the boats," 2000.

century ago Galway
fishermen looked
a photographer
facing balky gear
slow exposure
right in the eye posed
went back to work

knew tumblehome
deep curve of
their hooker's hull meant
safe rib coast return

they trusted as they
sailed blindly out
into the restless
necessary.

III. Unfamiliar Everyday

Unfamiliar Everyday

Elsewhere
maps lead to unpronounceable towns,
round signs show two squat cars
crossed out—no passing!—
and sinuous curves understate
the zigzagging narrow road
where stone walls stitch up hills
dotted with white sheep. Each time,
I experience it all anew.

Coming home feels
like exile to the known and gladly left.
Same small town, numbered streets,
same limited paths from here
to expected there and back, and back.

But wait. Leaves are changing fast.
Deep greens against sharp golds and reds,
flowers' fierce last burst of growth,
swift chill, heavy sky, a shift
from no coat to sweater to down.
Hugging myself against the wind,
I see. Sleeping bees
bead the bottom of late blossoms.
Leaves light the sidewalk.
As the sun warms, bees stir and rise,
begin their work of gathering
the season's last sweetness.
Keep your heart open.
Remember surprise.

Waiting

Flow of syrup from a bottle,
amber honey from a spoon,
the slow drip of sap
from a tapped maple in spring.
A jumpy old film, errant memory,
one moment yanked to another,
gaps that logic can't fill.

Over time the mind skitters and skids.

Wool-gathering, as if the skein
of attention might be woven
into a tidy pattern, might clothe
someone, keep them warm.

Waiting so wholly derails
whatever time might yield.
Clocks, dog walks, thoughts all
knot into sluggish now,
time pulses through each far-flung nerve
and vein and sense of the body
knit in an unforeseen design

as if I am the wool, a long piece
of thread in a heedless hand
unsure of a beginning or end.

Knowing

When the body is a burden how
do you say goodbye
to those who know you through it?

Who think you are what they see
or hold while you
know, you know,
in every weakening clasp

that you are already outside this
feeling your way beyond
bone and sinew seeking

that thread like an egg's anchor
that ties you to something else or

maybe I have that wrong

that unties you
from this frailing form
to become whatever unbodied thing

knows how to leave gracefully.

Hotel

Tidy gravestones blossom on Minnesota hillsides.
Limestone portal tombs rise across the green Irish countryside.
Carved angels stand in overgrown London cemeteries
where red foxes sleep on toppled, sun-warmed gravestones.
In catacombs and ossuaries, piled skulls, long leg bones,
tiny hand bones tangle and decorate dark passages.
Memorials rise to unnamed heroes. Odes remember.

The thing that remains is the gesture. The thing that is gone
flits away, won't stay in the stone, the wall, the ground,
in the prepared place, a hotel guest just passing through.
The rest of us tidy the room, make the bed, do the chores,
remain rooted in the everyday.

Confirmation

Like when you look closely—
maybe a guest is coming
so you are cleaning—
oh, a revelation of just what
you thought your house did not admit,
such neglect you are ashamed
and, yes, hear your mother's voice
and have seldom felt so far from grace.

How much do you miss every day?
What signs reveal your carelessness
in illuminated glory, bold script scrolling
across everyone's screen, breaking news,
proclaiming your offenses?

Like believing, really believing,
deep in your scrubbing hands,
that redemption is possible,
that given the right ritual
you can catechize all into clarity.

Like seeing, even as you scour,
that you touch only the grimy surface,
that your sacramental effort reveals
in return for that brief penance
only your warped metallic reflection—
still the same, still you, still you.

Ethics

A dead baby rabbit
eyes not open yet
in the garden
in the old leaves
something about the red
caught my attention

a snow shovel carries it
already stiffening
to the pile of branches
in the back and I see another
like a small brownish glove
carry it too out of sight

past stone markers for two beloved dogs
three dear cats, some orphaned kittens
and failed bird rescues,
my weeping children needing
on-the-spot pomp, a hymn or Disney song
to smooth the misstep of death

what to say for rabbits, squirrels, birds
spring-dazed and fallen
into our lives

yesterday two racing robins
sped past me right into a storefront window
crashed to the sidewalk shuddering
one died with a gasp the other staggered up
straightened its wings and walked away

so many small disasters we tidy up
even the language here removes me
from fault or act or decision
or whatever might be right

I put the shovel away
I go to work

Trigger Warning

as if the cause
sits precise and mechanical
set off with surety
to explode on cue

as if the link
between chaotic world
and quick-firing heart
might be listed
contained defined
in naming the noun
and avoidance enough

as if safety lay in silencing

verbs always act
the startling spark
ricochet of unruly emotions
nerves firing hair rising
the body's instinctive reply

imagine the blast of a gun close by
imagine the straight line
trigger to explosion to burst
of streaming synaptic fires
the syntax straightforward
the effects certain
in each thudding heart
and trembling encased brain

remember the work of words
remember nouns and verbs
things and their actions
and the body always the body
coping with all it must learn

remove your itching fingers
lace them into a bowl
and hold it open

Colors

The painter is still painting
the outside of my little house.
It is taking forever—
supply chain, his complicated life,
endless Minnesota weather.
Now, as I watch him
perched atop the ladder
painting deep chrome green window frames
in the midst of the maples'
bright, short-lived, glorious
red-gold leaves
I think it is precisely
the right timing.

Precarious Mechanics

Here's to the precarious mechanics of the body
as they resign their symbiotic tasks—
waving cilia of the ear and lung,
shedding skin, pulsing capillaries, stringy ligaments,
even the bacteria thronging each outpost -
they fail or rebel, balance falters,
the body becomes unpredictable and odd.

My father wonders why he has trouble walking.
The doctor says, "You're 94." But he remembers
the deep reach of stride, and we remember
the thrill when he would grasp a lamppost,
fling his legs up and out and hold himself horizontal.
Even as children, we saw the whim and strength of it.

Now my leg hurts, cilia grow stiff and thin,
joints prefer not to; the body becomes balky,
and I find no force to restart that green fuse
but my father's inspired optimism
and the vision of his body
horizontal over the sidewalk,
held by muscle and will against the inevitable
call of gravity.

The Past Tense Will Break Your Heart

easy to fall walking into the sea
against invisible undertow
across hidden jagged reefs

until beyond the breakers
land drops away and you float suspended
vast sky above and dark deep below

go farther tighten the plastic mask
seal the snorkel with your lips
tip your face down into the water
a world appears sunlit dense
goldgreen seaweed cratered red reefs delicate white coral

no sound, no vertical or horizontal,
only here now movement
everywhere in the breathing sea:
plants stirred by sudden bright fish -
slow orange grazers, sharp round yellows,
thin black with silver stripes, gusts
of quick small synchronized blue so close
they brush your wondering skin -
an eel, jaws wide, surges up and retracts,
a sea turtle like a small island grazes over the rocks -

this world unspools with no beginning or end
surrounds you suspends you transports you
until you pick up your head
abruptly air light sound startle you
waves crash people talk gulls laugh sun burns
and you wonder how long you might stay
where nothing needs to change
where all is quiet peace slow calm

that vision buoys you as sun stains the clouds
over the silvered water as you gather
to say goodbye as ukulele chords drift into the sky
as your brother's ashes sink slowly
into the dark waters that you know now
hold whole worlds

later you wonder if you can learn
to say his name in the past tense
and whether you have to—

Daylight Savings

A season's end is so clear:
collapsing jack-o'-lanterns,
chilled grass crouching low,
tall dried stalks of prairie plants
pointing at the heavy sky,
the mournful calls of geese
who no longer migrate
but know now is time to regroup.

Falling back an hour gives
a hint of coming repetitions,
the months of cold and ice, bursts
of snow halting everything.
One more hour, time
to rake leaves, wind hoses,
put on storm windows,
fortify against outside.

Already the house feels less open.
Already the door seems a narrow portal
from one world to its opposite.
Soon the house lights will beckon
in the early dark. Soon
piles of boots will gather by the door,
closets fill with puffy down coats,
mittens endlessly marry and separate.
The geese will stay by the lakes,
ducks stand on the frozen river.
Time seems to stop for months.

So give us tonight this hour back
to lie in the dark, consider what comes next,
replay sixty short minutes as rehearsal
for the long, looming hours of uncertain change
that we cannot save up for enough.

Return Again

Go back to the place
where rounded hills rise
deep greens and rocky peaks
beaded with soft white sheep
where dry limestone walls
stitch the landscape
into erratic patchwork
edged by endless gray blue seas
where you feel at once
at home, though you
never lived here.

Stand on a high point
at the end of a single-lane twister
of narrow heart-stop road
edging up the sharp mountain
stand wind-blasted and heart-spun
and read an Irish poem aloud,
words rushing into the rain-bright air.

Gulls' cries and wind's song
scattered words and distant cars
aching sound-shards of yearning
disperse into the embracing landscape
curving around and away.

You can always come back.
You can never leave.
Close your eyes. Wherever you are,
may these set-down words
held in place in a white space
carry you, heart-hopeful
and heart-worn you, home.

Susan Jaret McKinstry has published poems in *Plain Songs I & II, Crosswinds, Willows Wept, Red Wing Poet Artist Collaboration,* and *The Journal of General Internal Medicine.* A professor of 19th century British literature, theory, and creative writing at Carleton College in Northfield, Minnesota, she yearns for the sea, and has been lucky to teach in Ireland, Scotland, Norway, London, Florence, and Moscow.